A–Z

OF

IPSWICH

PLACES – PEOPLE – HISTORY

Sarah E. Doig

AMBERLEY

First published 2018

Amberley Publishing
The Hill, Stroud, Gloucestershire, GL5 4EP
www.amberley-books.com

Copyright © Sarah E. Doig, 2018

The right of Sarah E. Doig to be identified as
the Author of this work has been asserted in
accordance with the Copyrights, Designs and
Patents Act 1988.

ISBN 978 1 4456 8031 6 (print)
ISBN 978 1 4456 8032 3 (ebook)

British Library Cataloguing in Publication Data.
A catalogue record for this book is available
from the British Library.

Origination by Amberley Publishing.
Printed in Great Britain.

Contents

Introduction

When I was growing up in Bury St Edmunds on the 'other side' of Suffolk, Ipswich seemed a far-off, mysterious place full of ancient properties, industrial buildings that had seen better days and concrete jungles. So, what is a West Suffolk girl doing writing a book about Ipswich? Well, since my return to Suffolk, after a gap of around twenty-five years and with a new-found passion for history, I have been relearning the heritage of our county and exploring hitherto unknown parts of it. I have therefore had the pleasure of unlocking Ipswich's mysteries and have written this book with a fresh pair of eyes on its distinguished past. I hope you enjoy reading my *A–Z of Ipswich* as much as I have enjoyed writing it.

What particularly attracted me to this A–Z series of books was that they are not all about the words. The photographs are equally important, if not more so. The pictures are a way into the text; a passageway, if you like, from the present back to the past. I therefore asked my friend and experienced photographer Tony Scheuregger to work alongside me and to take all the wonderful photos you see in this book. Some of my requirements were for the mundane, illustrative photograph, but for others, I allowed him to be more adventurous. So, I am sure you will agree that when you turn the pages the photos inspire you to read and learn more about the county town of Suffolk.

A

Abolitionists

There is a blue plaque that sits well above head height on a rather down-at-heel building on the corner of St Matthew's Street and Portman Road. The plaque commemorates Richard Dykes Alexander (1788–1865), who is described as a Quaker, banker, philanthropist and pioneer photographer. Alexander had this building constructed in around 1840 as his out-of-town residence. He also owned a large swathe of land adjacent to his house to the north-west. As a Quaker, Richard Dykes Alexander was a pacifist and was therefore deeply concerned for the social welfare of the working population of Ipswich. Alexander was also a devoted supporter of the abolition of slavery. So, in the 1850s when Alexander made his land available

The blue plaque to an Ipswich philanthropist on Alexander House.

for housing, he stipulated that some of the streets should be named after leading abolitionists.

One of the best known of those who led the fight to abolish slavery was Thomas Clarkson, a devout Anglican and friend of Richard Dykes Alexander. Clarkson spent the last thirty years of his life living at Playford Hall, just outside Ipswich. Thomas Clarkson had campaigned against the slave trade since his Cambridge University days, where, in 1785, he won a Latin essay competition with a composition entitled (in English) 'Is it lawful to enslave the unconsenting?' The essay was subsequently published in English and was therefore able to reach a wider audience. It had a strong influence on an existing group of Members of Parliament sympathetic to the cause and, in May 1787, the Committee for the Abolition of the Slave Trade was formed. Thomas Clarkson took a leading role in the committee, collecting evidence to support the abolitionists' cause. He encouraged an Anglican MP, William Wilberforce, to join the group. Wilberforce was responsible for introducing the Abolition Bill before Parliament. After initial failures, legislation abolishing slavery was passed in 1807.

Today, the well-known names of Clarkson and Wilberforce can be seen side by side in Ipswich in the streets named after them. Other lesser-known abolitionists such as Anthony Benezet, William Dillwyn and Granville Sharp are also commemorated in nearby street names.

Two anti-slavery campaigners commemorated in street names.

Ancient House

If any one building is said to represent Ipswich's history and heritage more than any other, it is the Ancient House. It stands on the corner of the Buttermarket and St Stephen's Lane, and can boast of a colourful past. The house is thought to date back to the fifteenth century, but its best-known owners were the Sparrowe family, who owned the building for over 200 years; indeed, its alternative name is Sparrowe's House. As with all residential properties across the centuries, the Ancient House has been subject to remodelling and upgrading by subsequent owners. George Copping, who bought the property in the 1560s, substantially readapted or rebuilt the house in the typical Tudor timber-frame and plaster style. In 1603, the Ancient House then passed into the hands of William Sparrowe and it was his descendent Robert Sparrowe who stamped his mark firmly on the house.

Robert Sparrowe was a Royalist in a town that was strongly Puritan. The English Civil Wars, which began in 1642, divided the country between those who supported the monarchy and those who were, essentially, opposed to the divine rule of kings. After the execution of Charles I in 1649, the country was ruled by a Puritan parliament, and men like Sparrowe had to keep their Royalist sympathies well hidden. However, in 1660 the monarchy was restored. Robert Sparrowe was able to demonstrate his allegiance once again. In celebration of the Restoration, he gave his house a facelift and added a splendid royal coat of arms as well as a highly decorated plaster façade, known as pargetting. Among the illustrations that adorn the front are the four continents (Australia had not been discovered then). Asia is depicted by a domed, mosque-like building and a woman sitting on a horse. The figure for Africa is naked and sits holding a spear and parasol astride a crocodile.

The Ancient House never fails to impress residents and visitors alike.

Detail from the
Ancient House
pargetting – Asia.

Detail from the
Ancient House
pargetting – Africa.

There is a curious tale about the Ancient House and its connection to Matthew Hopkins, the self-styled Witchfinder General who was responsible for the deaths of many accused witches in Suffolk. In 1645, a woman called Mary Lackland was burned at the stake for having killed her husband by witchcraft. Husband and wife had lived next door to the Ancient House. In 1997, long after the house had been turned into commercial premises, staff reported ghostly happenings. A medium was brought in who identified the presence of an unhappy female ghost, long since dead. Was it perhaps the spirit of Mary Lackland who roamed the shop? Many think so, especially given the name of the retail outlet, Lakeland.

B

Bacon, Nathaniel

When Nathaniel Bacon died in 1660, the Corporation of Ipswich granted the princely sum of £25 to his widow '... for the great paynes that her husband ... did take in the transcribing of several ancient records belonging to this towne'. Nathaniel Bacon was a member of the prominent East Anglian Bacon family and was a key figure in Ipswich political life in the mid-seventeenth century. He was a lawyer and achieved the highest legal position in the town, as its Recorder. Until then he had not lived in Ipswich but on being invited to take up the position he took up residence in the parish of St Margaret's. Bacon was also elected as Member of Parliament for Ipswich several times, serving in the Commonwealth period of government under Oliver Cromwell. Nathaniel Bacon was described as a 'pious, prudent learned man' and, indeed, his learning drove him to spend many years compiling a digest of all the rules under which Ipswich was governed. He painstakingly transcribed from ancient documents all the more important decisions that had been made concerning

Nathaniel Bacon's house in St Margaret's Green.

The Ipswich Society

NATHANIEL
BACON
1593-1660
Recorder of Ipswich
Parliamentarian
lived here
1642-1660

A blue plaque commemorates Bacon's contribution to Ipswich.

the governance of the town. The result was *The Annalls of Ipswiche: The Lawes Customs and Government of the Same*, which he completed in 1654. This book provides modern-day historians with a fascinating insight into the running of the town over the centuries.

In Bacon's *Annalls* we learn about appointments to the official town band. The earliest mention of the musicians is in 1538 when three 'waits' were each provided with an annual salary of 13 shillings and 4 pence. In Tudor times, any self-respecting town in the country would have its own band of waits. Their main role was to play music for official and civic occasions, often in processions or as part of pageants and plays. In 1587, John Betts and four other musicians were appointed as the new town waits. Their duties included patrolling the town from two in the morning until daylight, perhaps waking up residents on dark winter mornings by playing under their windows!

The house in St Margaret's Green in which Nathaniel Bacon lived now bears a blue plaque in commemoration of this statesman.

Barracks

Over the centuries, Ipswich has played an important role as a port of embarkation for troops headed overseas in times of war. From 1744 onwards, there was a succession of invasion scares, when France threatened the British mainland. Being a town of strategic importance, therefore, Ipswich was bolstered by soldiers stationed there, often in local hostelries. However, these reached capacity quickly, and so, at first, makeshift camps of wooden huts were set up to house the troops, most notably near Round Wood on either side of Rushmere Lane. Manoeuvres were carried out on nearby Rushmere Heath. This camp, of which all traces are long since gone, was known as the St Helen's Barracks and accommodated 8,000 soldiers.

In 1795, a permanent barracks for cavalry soldiers was built on a large, 9¼-acre site in St Matthew's parish, designed to accommodate 1,500 men. Aptly known locally as the Horse Barracks, they were filled first by the 2nd (or Queen's) Regiment of Dragoon Guards. A large parade ground was flanked to the east and west by brick barracks for the rank and file soldiers. An officer's mess stood to the north. The spacious accommodation, and no doubt the warm welcome by the town's residents, made Ipswich a popular posting for troops. During the Napoleonic Wars in the early 1800s, the camp was used as a military hospital for wounded soldiers. Other mounted regiments came and went at the Horse Barracks until the second half of the nineteenth

The gateposts are almost all that is left of the Horse Barracks.

The maltings at Stoke Bridge were also used as barracks.

century when it gave way to artillery units, including the Royal Field Artillery and the Royal Horse Artillery. The barracks site was sold to the Ipswich Corporation in the late 1920s, who built council homes on what are now Cecil Road and Geneva Road. The only visible signs of the barracks today are the entrance gateposts in Barrack Lane and a few sections of boundary walls in nearby gardens.

At the outbreak of the Napoleonic Wars in 1803, the large riverside maltings at Stoke Bridge was converted into barracks to accommodate more troops. It reverted to its original purpose when peace with France was declared.

Bells

Just to the south of Stoke Bridge stands a timber-framed former pub. Although it is now a business premises, a carved corner post offers a clue as to the previous name of the building, the Old Bell. It is thought to be one of the oldest surviving pub buildings in Ipswich and although it is hard to date precisely, its first appearance in surviving records was in 1639. It is possible, though, that the pub is considerably older than this. Its name may well refer to a bell foundry that existed in the area as early as the thirteenth century, and the pub could well have served the metalworkers employed there. Originally, the Old Bell Inn was a much larger structure, but part of the east end was demolished in the mid-nineteenth century to make way for Vernon Street.

In the second half of the seventeenth century, John Darbie from Kelsale established a bell foundry in St Clement's parish. He had a good reputation across the county and cast 158 bells for Suffolk churches between 1658 and 1691, including for the

Right: Is that a cat or a sea monster beneath the bell?

Below: Although now offices, the Old Bell Inn sign is still prominent.

The bells peal from the top of St Lawrence's Church tower.

Ipswich churches of St Mary at the Elms, St Mary-le-Tower and St Peter's. Darbie also fashioned six bells for his home parish church of St Clement's, which were later rehung by another Ipswich bellfounder, Alfred Bowell. Alfred's father, Henry, had been a shipwright in the town but with the decline of wooden shipbuilding in Ipswich, he turned to the manufacture and hanging of bells. The Bowell family business continued until the Second World War.

High up in the tower of St Lawrence's Church in Dial Lane hangs the oldest surviving ring of church bells in the world. In 2009, the bells rang out after having been silent for twenty-four years. They had been removed in 1985 when the tower was declared unsafe. After a successful fundraising campaign, the tower was restored and a new, steel bell frame installed to allow for change ringing. The bells themselves remain unmodified and still include their original clappers. They therefore sound exactly the same as they would have done when four of them were cast in the 1440s and the other was added in around 1490. The set of five bells are known as 'Wolsey's Bells' after Cardinal Thomas Wolsey who grew up in the town and who would have heard the peal. It is believed that Wolsey's wealthy and influential uncle, Edmund Daundy, may have commissioned one of the bells.

Clocks

Local newspaper the *Ipswich Journal* carried the following advertisement in 1720: 'This is to acquaint the curious that at the Great White Horse in Ipswich is to be seen Tho. Moore's most famous astronomical and musical clock, with new additions.' Nine years later, the same watchmaker placed an advert for another of his inventions: 'Whereas Thomas Moore ... has for many years observed the misfortunes which very frequently happen to pocket watches of all sorts by sometimes coming into unskilful hands and into the hands of servants ... this is to give notice that [he] has made up several curious silver and gold watches so curiously contrived that let the watch be wound which way they please, either to the right or left, they cannot fail of winding up the watch.' This entrepreneur and his descendants continued their clock and watchmaking business in the town and fashioned the clock with its unusual iron face for the church of St Margaret's in Ipswich. The clock is framed in stone, which bears the date 1737. It was however another forty-one years before Moore of Ipswich manufactured and installed the clock, now one of the oldest in the town. It continued to be wound by hand until 2017.

In January 1868, Ipswich residents celebrated the opening of their new town hall on the Cornhill with a week of festivities. The local newspapers described the structure as '... an ornament to the borough – a building of which the entire county may be proud'. This new town hall replaced an old Palladian-style building that had become too small to serve the rapidly expanding population of the town.

The unusual iron clock face on St Margaret's Church.

Despite a petition, the town hall has just one clock.

The design of its successor was made the subject of a competition with a prize of 100 guineas for the best scheme. A local builder, Edward Gibbons, carried out the construction, which cost £16,000. A few months before the grand opening, local people had petitioned the corporation for the new town hall to have two clocks, one set at Greenwich Mean Time and the other to 'Ipswich Time', which was five minutes later. The issue was hotly debated among the town's bigwigs who concluded that the one clock should show Greenwich Mean Time. Twelve years later the Statutes (Definition of Time) Act was passed in parliament, which imposed a standard time across the country.

Cobbold Family

Ipswich simply would not be the place it is today without having benefitted from the Cobbold family. They were landowners in the town and the surrounding area. Christchurch Park was donated to the people of Ipswich by the Cobbolds. They also gave to the borough of Ipswich the land used, until 1911, for the Ipswich racecourse. The family also provided several Members of Parliament for the town as well as chairmen of Ipswich Town Football Club. However, perhaps the Cobbold family's main claim to fame is their brewing empire.

In 1746, Thomas Cobbold moved his Harwich brewery to Ipswich. Up until then, he had been transporting the crystal-clear water from the natural springs on his land at Holywells in Ipswich to use for the brewing process. In the end, it seemed sensible to move his operation to where his water supply was. He therefore bought some land at a spot known as the Cliff, beside the River Orwell and close to Holywells, and built a brewery and new family home. This business steadily grew under successive generations of Cobbolds and expanded into ship owning. John Cobbold, a third-generation Cobbold, took over the family empire and built Holywells House overlooking the springs. In 1825, John Cobbold took the family in a new direction by branching out into banking.

One of John Cobbold's grandsons, John Chevallier Cobbold, was one of the family's politicians. Having studied law, he returned to Ipswich and held several local government positions before being elected as one of the town's Members of Parliament, a position he held for twenty years. He and his father, John, were involved in the formation of the Eastern Union Railway that brought the railway to Ipswich for the first time. John Chevallier Cobbold also took a leading role in planning the Wet Dock and became one of the dock's commissioners. By the time the dock was opened in 1842, he was Mayor of Ipswich. When he died in 1882, one of the local newspapers said that he was '... so closely mixed up with the social and public life of the town as to be inseparable from the actual identity of Ipswich'.

In 1957, the Cobbold Brewery merged with the Tollemache Brewery to form Tolly Cobbold. From 1977, it experienced successive takeovers and acquisitions until their

The Cliff Brewery and Cobbold family home have seen better days.

great rivals, Greene King, acquired Ridley's in 2005. With this move, the last surviving Tolly Cobbold beer, Tolly Original, ceased to be produced. The Cobbold's banking interests continued in various guises into the twentieth century. The Cobbold family sold the Holywells estate in 1930, which was subsequently bequeathed to Ipswich Town Council. Sadly, John Cobbold's Holywells mansion was demolished in 1962 due to an infestation of wood rot.

Cornhill

To tell the story of the Cornhill is to relive the history of Ipswich from very earliest times. It is named after the trade in grain, transacted there across the centuries, but the origins of the Cornhill go back further in time. The ruling family of East Anglia from around AD 550 was the Wuffingas who claimed to be descended from both Julius Caesar and Woden, one of the main pagan gods. Their chief seat of power was at Rendlesham, but it is thought that there was a royal residence on the Cornhill in Ipswich. There was also an early church there, named after St Mildred, which probably dated from the seventh or eighth centuries. Sometime in the 1500s, the building stopped being used as a church and became the seat of local government. It became known as the moot hall or guildhall. Some of this structure survived until 1812 when it was pulled down. The town hall, opened in 1867, now sits on this site.

Another key feature of the Cornhill was the market cross. The first market cross was erected in 1510 with money given by a wealthy merchant, Edmund Daundy. It is

There is some fine detailing on buildings in the Cornhill.

possible that its purpose then was as a place to preach sermons. A second, more elaborate market cross replaced it in around 1628. This was an octagonal structure and had a lead-clad roof. This lasted until 1812 when it was decided to demolish it '… in furtherance of the improvements that were then taking place'. The Cornhill at this time must have been very busy. Corn trading was still taking place, as well as the buying and selling of all manner of livestock. There had been a timber-framed 'shambles' on one side of the Cornhill, where butchers plied their trade. This had briefly been replaced by a rotunda in 1794, which lasted only sixteen years. A corn exchange was later built on this site, which was, in turn, swept away by a new building in 1880 that was to serve as the post office.

The now former post office is a monument to Victorian civic architecture and is adorned by elaborate decorative features and by sculptures. Four of the more prominent sculptures represent concepts very much at the cutting edge of nineteenth-century industrial life, namely industry, steam, electricity and commerce.

In 2018, work began once more to transform the Cornhill, this time as a place fit for twenty-first-century living. The new-look Cornhill will feature a main plinth, green granite tiled slabs and four celebratory columns inspired by the figures on the former post office and those on the town hall. Ambient lighting, benches and trees will also be installed.

The figure representing steam on the former post office.

Dial Lane

The present-day narrow alleyway called Dial Lane, boasting the magnificent tower of St Lawrence's Church, has undergone a number of name changes across the centuries and has, therefore, lost its medieval associations. There is, however, one clue as to one of its previous incarnations. On the east side of St Lawrence's Church there is a carved stone panel depicting a large pair of tailor's shears. Until 1447, the area around the church was known as the cloth market. At this time, Ipswich was a prosperous major trading centre for all manner of goods and produce, and one of its most important trades was in cloth, where Ipswich-woven cloth was sold alongside cloth from further afield in Suffolk as well as Essex. In 1448, in recognition of its importance to the town, the authorities decreed that all clothiers were to sell their cloth each market day at the moot hall (which stood in the Cornhill) and not elsewhere. These merchants therefore moved their base along the road, leaving the current Dial Lane to reinvent itself.

Draper's shears on the wall of St Lawrence's Church.

Ghosts of the past in Dial Lane?

With the clothiers gone, the lane was occupied by the medieval equivalent of fast food shops, selling hot pasties and pies. Only the wealthiest Ipswich residents had kitchens in their houses, and so these food shops were popular and therefore profitable. The lane therefore became known as Cook(e)'s Row. It kept this name until the eighteenth century when, after briefly being called the Buttermarket, it was called St Lawrence Lane.

By the nineteenth century Dial Lane had taken on its new identity. It was renamed simply because of a large clock that projected into the street from the tower of St Lawrence. In 1882, the unstable tower was rebuilt, and the clock removed. However, the name of the street remained.

Dickens, Charles

Arguably the most famous Victorian author of all time was a frequent visitor to Suffolk. Like many other writers, Charles Dickens drew inspiration for his characters and plots from the places he frequented and the people he observed. In *The Pickwick Papers*, which was published first in monthly instalments in 1836 and 1837, Dickens used the Great White Horse on Tavern Street as the backdrop for a scene where Mr Pickwick accidently enters the bedroom of a middle-aged lady. Dickens describes the inn as 'this overgrown tavern', which he said was known in the neighbourhood for its size '... in the same degree as a prize ox, or county paper-chronicled turnip, or unwieldy pig'. His Mr Pickwick loses himself in the Great White Horse's 'labyrinths

Above: Scene of Mr Pickwick's exploits.

Right: On subsequent visits to the town, Dickens did not stay here!

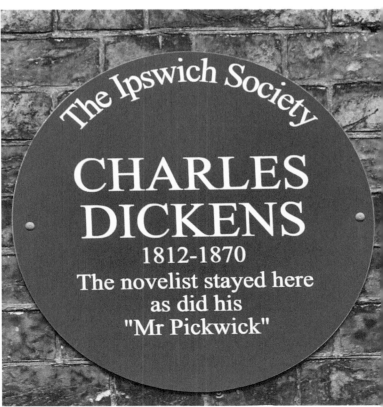

The Ipswich Society

CHARLES DICKENS

1812-1870

The novelist stayed here
as did his
"Mr Pickwick"

of uncarpeted passages' and 'clusters of mouldy, ill-lighted rooms'. Needless to say, Charles Dickens did not stay at the Great White Horse when in Ipswich again. In fact, the proprietor of the tavern, William Brooks, threatened to sue the novelist for what he considered a libellous description.

Two of the characters in *The Pickwick Papers* were based on Ipswich folk. Mrs Elizabeth Cobbold, second wife of John Cobbold the brewer, was the inspiration for Mrs Leo Hunter who mirrored Elizabeth Cobbold's love of poetry. The stagecoach driver, Tony Weller, in the book was based on John Cole, who was the last coachman to try to compete with the railways.

Charles Dickens returned to Ipswich several times during his career to give readings of his works for which he drew large audiences. In October 1859, he held a reading at the old corn exchange building where he read from *A Christmas Carol* as well as from *The Pickwick Papers*. In November 1861 Dickens was at the corn exchange again, this time reading *David Copperfield* in six chapters. The *Ipswich Journal* reporting the event said that his reading to a packed house was '... calm, gentlemanly and quite without mannerism or artificial effect and every passage tells upon the audience simply by virtue of the excellence that is in it'.

Drama and Dance

In the late 1500s and early 1600s, Ipswich was visited ten times by a troupe of actors from London called the Lord Chamberlain's Men, later called the King's Men or His Majesty's Players. Its most notable member was a young William Shakespeare, who wrote some of the plays they performed. On their first visit in 1594, the town paid the company 40 shillings per performance, four times as much as many other troupes and twice as much as the Queen's Men, the main provincial touring company. It is almost certain that Shakespeare came with his troupe to Ipswich, when they were possibly joined by the town's waits (musicians) who would have provided the music that was central to many of Shakespeare's plays. Ipswich residents had to wait a further century before their first permanent theatre was built in Tacket Street.

The centre of social life in Georgian Ipswich was the assembly house or assembly rooms. This was where the well-to-do could meet at the card table or attend balls. These balls, along with plays and concerts, were often held to coincide with the annual horse races in May and June. No doubt the cream of Ipswich society thought themselves adept on the dance floor. This was, sadly, not a view held by a visiting Frenchman, François de la Rochefoucauld, who toured Suffolk in 1784. He recorded, 'The two sexes dance equally badly, without the least grace, no steps, no rhythm. The women hold themselves badly, the head hanging forward, the arms dangling, the eyes lowered, the men with their knees bent; they suddenly change direction with their legs; in short their appearance is most disagreeable as they dance.' Undeterred by such remarks, and finding the then assembly rooms inadequate, new assembly rooms in Northgate Street were constructed. They opened with a ball and supper in January 1821, which was attended by nearly 200 of the nobility and gentry of the county. Sadly, in a matter of years, financial problems led to the building being sold. It has since had a number of incarnations including housing the Ipswich High School for Girls.

The old Northgate Street Assembly Rooms awaiting yet another transformation.

Egerton, Reginald

If you look closely, Ipswich's buildings reveal tantalising clues about premises and businesses that have long since disappeared from the town's streets. One of these is a large painted sign on a wall that simply reads: 'Egertons (Ipswich) Ltd 100 yds'. It also bears the British Petroleum (BP) logo and an arrow which points along Crown Street. When freshly painted, this sign would have been highly visible to motorists driving through town from the east. Although the sign does not bear a date, it is possible to hazard a guess as to when, roughly, it was painted by tracking through the history of one of the best-known pioneers of the motor industry in Britain.

The firm has its origins in the nineteenth century when an engineer named William Botwood established a coach-building business in 1875. The company went from strength to strength under William's sons when around seventy-five different types of carriage, ranging from rickshaws to gigs and shooting wagons, were exported all over the world. Botwoods quickly saw the potential in the new motor vehicle and by the turn of the century were doing good business selling car bodies. In 1902, Justin Reginald

The motor car showroom has long since disappeared.

'Reggie' Egerton joined them, and the company name changed to Botwood & Egerton motor engineers. Disagreements between the Botwoods and Egerton led to a split in 1910 and Reggie set up his own rival company in Northgate Street, opening new premises in Crown Street in 1928. After a series of takeovers and amalgamations, Egerton's Crown Street showroom became surplus to requirements. It was sold and demolished to make way for a new swimming and leisure facility.

Reggie Egerton was a colourful character who promoted the car in its early days, when many people regarded the invention with suspicion and fear. In 1904, Reggie was convicted by Ipswich magistrates of driving in a manner dangerous to the public in Princes Street. He appealed against his conviction and his appeal was upheld. It is therefore believed that Egerton's appeal was the first ever successful appeal against the new Motor Car Act.

Electric House

Perhaps one of the best-known buildings in Ipswich, usually as a landmark or reference point for shoppers or those meeting friends, is Electric House. It stands boldly at the top of Lloyds Avenue, forming an island of its own between a car park, bus station and a busy road. Electric House was built by the Ipswich Corporation in 1933 in the art deco style of the age. It was the purpose-built headquarters of the Ipswich Electricity Supply Centre, which became renowned for its bright

An art deco gem in the town centre.

floodlighting, neon signs and bold lettering draped around the building, and would have been quite a sight in its heyday.

With a steel construction and faced with reconstructed stone, many of the wonderful details commissioned of the stonemasons for the Electric House façade can barely be discerned from street level. The crest of the electricity company is emblazoned with its intertwined acronym IESC, and topped with a banner proclaiming 'LIGHT POWER HEAT'. There are also false pillars with motifs such as zigzag lightning, fan-shaped lights and pointed stars. Electric House was also the site of the exciting launch, in 1975, of Radio Orwell, the first commercial radio station to broadcast from Ipswich. Radio Orwell later merged with Saxon Radio to become SGR FM (and later Heart Ipswich). In 2017, an Ipswich property company unveiled fourteen new, 'Manhattan-style' apartments, along with a roof terrace, in the converted building.

Lloyds Avenue, which leads down from Electric House to the Cornhill, was also constructed in the 1930s and included the Odeon cinema (now the Mecca bingo hall), which opened in 1936. This building also has a distinctive art deco frontage where the ghost of the original 'ODEON' wording can be seen above the pillars. At the back of the building there is a plain brick wall with a single white brick. This commemorates a building worker who fell to his death during construction, the white brick marking the spot where he was working when he fell.

The ghost of the words ODEON can just be seen above the pillars.

F

Fore Street

On 21 July 1961, Elizabeth II visited Ipswich to open the newly built Civic College, which stood off Grimwade Street. After the opening ceremony, the royal motorcade travelled along almost the whole length of Fore Street. The street is one of the ancient thoroughfares of the town, linking the docks with the eastern parts of the town centre. Many of the buildings in the street are of historical interest but were in a bad state of repair. Therefore, in advance of the royal visit, an extensive improvement scheme was launched, inspired by the Ipswich Society. On the face of it, it seemed an undertaking driven by vanity. When Elizabeth I made a summer progress through East Anglia in 1578, Norwich prepared for the royal visit in a similar way, with frenzied activity to level and gravel the roads, paint the market cross and to remove the public pillory from the marketplace.

In the Elizabethan era, Fore Street would have been a bustling, happening place to be. Wealthy merchants set up home in fantastic timber-framed dwellings.

There are many fine, timber-framed buildings in Fore Street.

Fore Street at its very best.

Thomas Eldred, a merchant and mariner, lived in Fore Street and achieved the second English circumnavigation of the globe between 1586 and 1588. Many of the Tudor houses became pubs and inns in later centuries, including the former Neptune Inn. The building dates back to the fifteenth century and the date 1639, painted on the front, probably refers to a restyling. It could have been then that a merchant's house became an inn.

The work carried out during the Fore Street facelift for Elizabeth II's visit was far from just cosmetic; it greatly improved the road and pavements. It also probably saved several historic buildings from major structural disrepair. The Ipswich Society's vision, therefore, has ensured that future generations can appreciate the heritage of one of Ipswich's foremost streets.

Freehold Land Society

The Victorian era saw Ipswich expand rapidly. In 1801, the population of the town had been 11,000, but 100 years later it had increased six-fold to 66,000. The opening of the wet dock in 1842 had allowed, for the first time, larger vessels to reach the quay, paving the way for commercial and industrial success. Middle-class suburbs appeared as the well-to-do put down roots in the town. However, there was a need for more affordable homes and coupled with the Reform Act of 1832, there was demand for houses for ordinary workers. This legislation provided a way for the working man to have a vote for the first time. Anyone who owned a property valued at 40 shillings or more was able to vote, and so a national movement to create 'forty shillings freeholders' was born.

The semi-detached villas where Foxhall Road meets Back Hamlet.

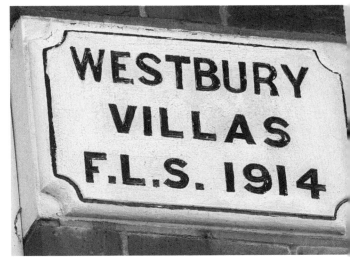

Freehold Land Society plaques can be seen dotted around the town.

The Ipswich & Suffolk Freehold Land Society was formed in 1849 and it bought up large estates and areas of land on the outskirts of Ipswich (as well as elsewhere in the county). They divided the land up into smaller parcels and built residential accommodation on them, each plot just big enough to qualify under the 40-shilling rule. A ballot was then held for members of the society, and those successful in the ballot were entitled to buy the property (with the assistance of a mortgage). The scheme was hugely popular and in some cases as many as 1,000 people entered the ballot for just forty plots.

Some of the first Ipswich houses built by the Freehold Land Society were in 1866 in Lancaster Road, and comprised what were described as 'high-quality, 2-bedroom, workman's houses'. In Palmerston Road, the society built and sold 'pretty and substantial six-room cottages'. Many other houses followed, including in Bramford Road, Nacton Road and Foxhall Road. Dotted around the town you can spot some plaques on houses bearing the acronym FLS, indicating that the homes were built and sold by the Freehold Land Society.

Although the Freehold Land Society itself was wound up in 1965, its mortgage arm continued and today is known as the Ipswich Building Society.

Friars

Medieval Ipswich was dominated by its churches. Religion was part of everyday life for the town's inhabitants who would have worshipped at their parish church. Another feature of religious activity was the preaching of the friars. These men devoted themselves to a life of poverty and self-sacrifice as well as helping the needy in society. Three separate orders of preaching friars set up religious communities in Ipswich in the thirteenth century. These friaries were extensive, with living, sleeping and eating accommodation as well as a large church in which to preach.

There is very little left of the Ipswich friaries today. The one exception is the excavated remains of the church of the Dominican friars, which lies between Foundation Street and Lower Orwell Street. The Dominican order of friars was also known as Blackfriars. Their church was dedicated to St Mary and had a length of 54 metres. Soon after the Dissolution of the Monasteries by Henry VIII, this church was demolished, and the other friary buildings were put to other uses.

What remains of Blackfriars Friary is now a Scheduled Ancient Monument.

The Whitefriars, or Carmelites, founded a friary in 1278–79 to the south of the Buttermarket. They further extended their community in the fourteenth century, which was bounded by the Buttermarket, Falcon Street, Queen Street and St Stephen's Lane. Henry VI and his court were accommodated in the friary on a visit to Ipswich in 1452. Some of the Whitefriars buildings survived until the nineteenth century and excavations on the site in 1987 revealed remains of the church, the cloister and the chapter house.

The third friary was that of the Franciscans or Greyfriars. Today in Ipswich, the name is synonymous with a twentieth-century attempt at development which backfired. The friary was established close to St Nicholas' Church on a riverside site. Some buildings survived into the seventeenth century, but they had long since disappeared when the planners got their hands on the site in the mid-1960s. They built new roads, a roundabout, pedestrian underpasses, a car park, retail units, flats and offices, all in the hope that traders and shoppers would move to this exciting new development. Few did move their business there. The market was also moved to Greyfriars but was a disaster. In the mid-1980s, Willis, Faber & Dumas took over much of the site. Shopping units were demolished and the area was landscaped.

The market is now back in and around the Cornhill.

Giles, Carl

There is a rather unusual statue that has pride of place in the centre of Ipswich. While to the younger generation it may mean nothing at all, to others, the group of figures is instantly recognisable as the Giles family. There is the spiky-haired Grandma wielding her umbrella, Aunt Vera with her constantly runny nose and remarkably thin ankles, and the twins in their matching bobble hats who are feeding sausages to the dog. The family were the creation of a man who was voted, in 2000, Britain's favourite cartoonist. He was Ronald 'Carl' Giles and, although he was born in Islington, spent the vast majority of his working life in Ipswich. Giles first moved to the town to work as an animator at a studio in Museum Street. During the Second World War, Carl Giles joined the Express Group and, for the next half a century, drew cartoons for the *Daily Express* and *Sunday Express*. He chronicled the whole gamut of British life through his regular cartoons in these papers, often using the Giles family he had invented to show the man in the street's view of the news. His adopted home town features in many of Giles' cartoons, such as his local pub, the Fountain in Tuddenham, the (then) Cornhill police station and St Lawrence's Church tower. His original cartoons are now sought after by collectors.

This bronze statue was sponsored by Express Group Newspapers and sculpted by Ipswich-born Miles Robinson. It was unveiled in 1993 in the presence of Carl

Giles' Grandma.

The twins feed sausages to the dog.

Giles himself. Sadly, it was vandalised in the early years but in 2010 it was resited, with added plinth, in a prominent position where Buttermarket, Princes Street and Queen Street meet. Aptly, Grandma is looking up at the studio window of the former East Suffolk House where Giles used to work.

Gipeswic

Ipswich was founded in the late sixth or early seventh century on the north bank of the River Orwell, one of a number of small Anglo-Saxon settlements near where the River Gipping flows into the Orwell. Ipswich emerged as a 'wic' or 'emporium' – essentially a port that traded goods with similar centres across the North Sea, and so Gipeswic was formed. It is thought to be one of the oldest continuously inhabited towns in Britain, if not the oldest. Ipswich's early economy was based on manufacturing and in the eighth century, the most important industry was pottery-making. The so-called 'Ipswich-ware' supplied the whole of East Anglia, as well as further afield. Archaeological digs have established that the Anglo-Saxon town covered around 50 hectares (compared with today's sprawl to over 4,000 hectares). The early layout of the streets is also reflected in the modern-day road system. St Stephen's Lane, for example, follows the course of an Anglo-Saxon path alongside which postholes from timber-framed houses have been found. A crossing point on the River Orwell where Stoke Bridge is now allowed for access to a small part of the town south of the river.

As pagan practices gave way to widespread Christianity, it is likely that Ipswich had one or more places of worship, possibly on the site of some of its current

Above: St Mary at Stoke is probably a Domesday church.

Left: The ancient door at St Mary at the Elms.

churches. All traces of some of these early churches have long since disappeared, including St Mildred's, which stood on Cornhill and St Augustine's in Stoke. William the Conqueror's Domesday Book, compiled in 1086, records two Ipswich churches dedicated to St Mary. These are thought to be St Mary-le-Tower and St Mary at Stoke. The latter church stands in a prominent position near the foot of a ridge, just south-west of Stoke Bridge and the town centre. St Mary at the Elms is a later church built in the eleventh or twelfth century and its earliest surviving architectural feature is the remarkable main (south) door, which dates from around this time. It is possibly the original door, which would make it one of the earliest structures still in use for its original purpose in Suffolk.

Grammar

As a major trading centre in medieval times, Ipswich needed an educated workforce. Young men expecting to make their living as tradesman needed to be able to count and measure. Therefore, some local education provision was required, and boys were usually sent to a grammar school between the ages of nine and twelve. They would also learn Latin grammar as this was the language used in textbooks. Records of schooling in Ipswich date back to the early fifteenth century. The first recorded headmaster of the borough school was Richard Pynington. In 1412, Pynington was sued for assault by a local butcher. When the schoolmaster failed to appear in court, his goods were seized, including his academic gowns and grammar books.

When, in 1483, wealthy merchant Richard Felaw died, he left his house opposite the Blackfriars church in present-day Foundation Street as a permanent home for the town's grammar school. Then, at the height of his power, Cardinal Thomas Wolsey established a school in Ipswich in the late 1520s. The College of St Mary, as

Wolsey's Gate is all that is left of the cardinal's college dream.

Ipswich School was built in the 1850s in a mock-Elizabethan style.

it was called, was founded on the site of the dissolved priory of St Peter and St Paul, one of the many monasteries across the country that Wolsey had closed due to alleged corruption. Wolsey's school and the grammar school merged for just a short time. Cardinal Wolsey's fall from grace came in 1529 and he died the following year. His school was closed and largely demolished.

The grammar school in Ipswich re-emerged after Wolsey thanks to a number of endowments, moving back to the former Blackfriars site. It remained there until 1852 when it moved to new premises on Henley Road, overlooking Christchurch Park. Prince Albert had laid the foundation stone for these Elizabethan-style buildings, now known as the Ipswich School, on his visit to the town the previous year.

H

Humber Doucy Lane

Many Ipswich residents probably don't give a second thought to the rather unusual name of the road which forms part of the boundary between Ipswich and Rushmere. The area is best known by locals as the site of 150 prefabricated bungalows. These houses sprung up, in Ipswich and elsewhere in the country, in the years immediately following the Second World War. In 1944, Prime Minister Winston Churchill announced an extensive emergency temporary housing programme aimed at alleviating the housing shortage left in the wake of wartime enemy bombing. In total, some 156,000 prefabs were built across the country between 1945 and 1949. These prefab housing units were cheap, mass-produced aluminium or steel-framed units that arrived almost fully constructed from the factory. The frame of the Tarran bungalows in the Humber Doucy Lane area came with already constructed bolt-on concrete panels, which formed the walls. They also had a characteristic flat roof covered with bitumen felt. Although designed to last just ten or fifteen years, these houses in Ipswich are still used today.

So where did the unusual name of the lane come from? Well, like many other such names, we don't know for certain. However, during the Napoleonic Wars in the early 1800s, nearby Rushmere Heath was used as a camp for French prisoners of war. When these soldiers were marched along Humber Doucy Lane, it was said that they enjoyed the 'ombre douce' or 'sweet shade' of the hedges and trees that ran along the road. In time, this French nickname became the English Humber Doucy.

Interestingly, in 1930, H. O. Cox (Car Sales) Ltd of St Peter's Street, Ipswich, advertised an elegant new car called the Humber Doucy. Described as having graceful styling, exceptional visibility, complete luxury, deep seating and deluxe fittings, walnut facia and impeccable interior finish, and generous luggage space, the advert urged purchasers, 'Why not drive your brand new Humber Doucy along Humber Doucy Lane?' I wonder whether anyone did so?

There is not very much 'sweet shade' to be found here nowadays.

I

Iron

The name of Garretts is synonymous with the Industrial Revolution. In the eighteenth century, when road travel was becoming vital for industry and communications, turnpike trusts were set up by Acts of Parliament to manage stretches of road and to ensure the upkeep of the main highways. From 1767, milestones were compulsory on all such roads, not only to inform travellers of direction and distances, but to help coaches keep to schedule. At their height, there were over 200 milestones in Suffolk. Stone, however, was in short supply in the region and when the lettering on the stones became worn, cast-iron mileposts were made to attach to the existing stone. Many of these were manufactured in Ipswich at the ironworks of Jacob Garrett. These have lasted well, and you can spot a number along the route of the former Ipswich to Great Yarmouth Turnpike.

Below left: You can still see Garretts' iron milestones along Woodbridge Road.

Below right: Nothing remains of Robert Ransome's original foundry.

For nearly two centuries, Ransomes was probably the most famous Ipswich manufacturing name around the world and was a company at the heart of the industrial expansion of the town. Having served an apprenticeship to a Norwich ironmonger, Robert Ransome set up his own foundry in the city where he was granted a patent for a process to harden the surface of ploughshares. A few years later, Ransome moved to Ipswich where he established a foundry at St Margaret's Ditches, now Old Foundry Road. A further patent, granted in 1803, enabled the ironfounder to further improve the durability of ploughs. Through careful diversification of the business, which ranged from agricultural machinery to civil and railway engineering, Ransomes was the largest manufacturer of metal goods in the country by the mid-nineteenth century. Perhaps their most famous and enduring of products was the lawnmower. In the First World War the firm manufactured aeroplanes. The company, under various names, continued until 1998 when their independent existence ceased with a takeover by an American firm.

Isaac Lord's

The name Isaac Lord will be familiar to all those who live, work and study in or near the smart new Ipswich Waterfront. It is possible that many believe that the Isaac Lord complex, now a bar, restaurant and associated buildings, is named after the original

Isaac Lord was not the original owner of these historic buildings.

Part of this house dates from the fifteenth century.

owner of the historic buildings. In fact, it bears the name of one of the relatively recent custodians of the property. Isaac Lord bought the range of buildings from the famous Cobbold family in 1900, continuing the malting business there as well as trading coal and corn. After Isaac's death the firm continued until the 1980s and for a while, the building fronting the dock was used as a maritime museum before extensive restoration and refurbishment took place.

Isaac Lord's started life in the fifteenth and sixteenth centuries as a merchant's house and trading business. The half-timbered house, which has been dated to as early as 1478, faces Fore Street, and the warehouses face the wet dock. Merchandise would have been unshipped, stored and distributed wholesale, or sold retail in a shop attached to the house on the street front. The complex also had a sale room and a malt kiln. The whole property is said to be the best such example in the country.

Medieval Ipswich was one of only four authorised wool trade centres in East Anglia and the only one in Suffolk. The Isaac Lord buildings, therefore, would have been used for the export to Europe of the woollen finished cloth manufactured in Suffolk weaving villages. The sale room would have been used to auction imported goods.

J

Jews

Ipswich in the Middle Ages was a cosmopolitan town due to it being a centre for international trade. People of various nationalities and religious persuasions therefore settled there, thus contributing to the town's rich history. There was an early Jewish community in Ipswich, which is believed to have started in the second half of the twelfth century, in the reign of Henry II. It was one of twenty-six centres to have an *archa*, an official, lockable chest in which copies of all deeds and contracts involving Jews were deposited. This community, like many others in Britain, disappeared in the thirteenth century either before or shortly after 1290 when Edward I expelled all Jews from the country. Between then and their formal return, there is no official trace of Jews on English soil.

At Oliver Cromwell's invitation, Jews returned to England in 1656 and settled in London. During the Jacobite Rebellions, some Jews left London to establish trade in the

The old Jewish cemetery is well hidden.

port towns – Ipswich being one of these – and it is thought that a Jewish congregation was formed here around 1730. They met in a hired room in the parish of St Clement's. By the end of the eighteenth century the size of the Jewish population justified the construction of a synagogue. The foundation stone was laid on 18 August 1792 and contemporary accounts described it as a 'neat and commodious synagogue'. Four years later a small burial ground was acquired nearby when the Jewish community in Ipswich reached its peak. Relations with the rest of the town's population, though, had their ups and downs. Despite some disturbances outside the synagogue, Ipswich's market day was moved to Tuesday from its traditional Saturday – the Jewish holy day – so that Jewish traders could sell their goods. In the first half of the nineteenth century, the number of Jews in the town began to drop until, in the 1850s, there were just five Jewish families left. The synagogue was closed shortly after and was demolished in 1877. The burial ground had been closed in 1855 under the Burial Act, and a Jewish plot was acquired in the municipal cemetery for future burials. After the closure the burial ground fell into disrepair but in 1893 the London Committee (now Board) of Deputies of British Jews took over responsibility for maintenance of the site.

K

King Edward VIII

In 2016, a large Victorian desk was delivered into the safekeeping of the Ipswich Museum. It had been removed from the old Assize court in St Helen's Street in 1969 when the court was replaced with the Crown Court in Civic Drive. At first glance it may have seemed like just another piece of the town's long and fascinating history. It had formed part of the press benches in the court and, over the years, reporters covering cases had scratched their names on it. This piece of furniture, though, witnessed one of the greatest events in British history in the twentieth century.

In the autumn of 1936, Mrs Wallis Simpson spent six weeks living in Felixstowe to gain the necessary residential qualifications to have her divorce hearing held in Suffolk. Mrs Simpson was, of course, not just any potential divorcée. She was the woman that Edward VIII wanted to marry and, in order to do so, she needed to be free to marry. With the affair already in the public domain and the world's press hungry to follow developments, the Assize court in Ipswich was chosen for the divorce proceedings as it was hoped it would be a low-key event. However, the press had got wind of the pending case and, on 27 October, the town was besieged by reporters

The scene of historic divorce proceedings.

eager to report a royal public scandal. The police had closed off St Helen's Road to prevent photographers getting a glimpse of Mrs Simpson. The hearing lasted barely twenty-five minutes, after which time the judge, Mr Justice Hawke, granted Wallis Simpson a decree nisi. She was then driven at high speed to London. The hearing in Ipswich, though, led to a crisis, which was finally resolved two months later when Edward VIII abdicated his throne to be able to marry his fiancée.

Although the king visited Mrs Simpson while she was staying in Felixstowe, he was not at the divorce hearing. He had, however, visited Ipswich in 1930 when he was the Prince of Wales to open the new municipal aerodrome, which in time expanded to become Ipswich Airport.

L

Lady Lane

It is hardly surprising that many Ipswich residents are unaware of the historic importance of Lady Lane. Today, it is a mere passageway, a thoroughfare used by many to get from the car park to the town centre. It is therefore difficult to imagine how it might have looked in Tudor times. Then, it was a busy street that sat just outside the Westgate of the town. It had almshouses on either side of the road. More significantly, however, was the presence of a chapel which held a shrine to Our Lady of Grace – hence the street name. It was on the site where miracles were said to have taken place. It was a shrine to which monarchs came. In 1297, Princess Elizabeth, daughter of King Edward I, married the Count of Holland in Ipswich, and it is thought the ceremony took place at the shrine chapel. In 1517, Catherine of Aragon, Henry VIII's first wife, visited the shrine and then in 1522, Henry VIII himself prayed at the shrine in the hope of a miracle of a baby boy and heir to the throne. Because of this royal patronage, pilgrims from across the country and, probably further afield, flocked to pay homage at the shine of Our Lady.

Twenty-first-century Lady Lane is a shadow of its former self.

The 'Madonna of Ipswich' is the only clue to a once-great thoroughfare.

When Henry VIII broke from Rome and suppressed Catholic institutions, the shrine was closed. It is said that the original carved wooden statue of Our Lady from the shrine was taken to London to be burnt but was, instead, rescued by Catholic sailors and smuggled to Nettuno in Italy. However, although an ancient statue of Our Lady of the Graces still stands in a shrine in the Italian town, experts believe it is not the Ipswich statue.

Today, a small, metal replica statue affixed to a modern brick wall in Lady Lane is the only reminder of this once great place.

Listed Buildings

When we think of a listed building, we often conjure up in our mind a picturesque half-timbered house. However, listed-building status can be conferred on a whole range of different architectural styles, old and new. Ipswich has more than its fair share of listed buildings, many of which – possibly not surprisingly – are its ancient churches like St Mary at the Elms, which is designated as Grade II*. It is late eleventh or early twelfth century in origin and, like many of the town's churches, it has been altered, expanded and partly rebuilt numerous times during its life. The church has a brick tower that was built in the sixteenth century, one of the finest Tudor church towers in the county.

Another Grade II* property in Ipswich is Gippeswyk Hall, which was built in around 1600 as a farmhouse. Its layout mirrors other Elizabethan houses such as the much grander Christchurch Mansion. However, Gippeswyk Hall is slightly unusual in that it faces east rather than the more typical south. This is probably due to the slope that lies to the south. When the hall ceased to be a farmhouse

Above: The Tudor brick tower of St Mary at the Elms.

Below: The small but perfectly formed Elizabethan Gippeswyk Hall.

One of Foster Associates' earliest designs.

there was a succession of wealthy owners including a distinguished doctor, Sir Alfred Garrod. Garrod had begun his career at Ipswich Hospital in the mid-nineteenth century before moving to London. He was appointed physician-extraordinary to Queen Victoria in 1890.

The older the building is, the more likely it is to be listed and usually a building must be over thirty years old to be listed. However, one rare exception to this is the iconic Willis Building which, in 1991, became the youngest building in the country to be granted Grade I-listed status. The insurance brokers Willis, Faber & Dumas moved to Ipswich in the 1970s and commissioned Norman Foster to design a new office building. He was asked to design a building that would be sympathetic to human values. The £6.5 million construction was completed in 1975 and has a curved outer wall clad in bronze-tinted glass. The central escalators lead up to a rooftop staff restaurant and garden. There was also an Olympic-sized swimming pool for employees to use, although this was subsequently covered over, making way for more office space.

M

Memorials

Like many other towns in Britain, Ipswich lost many hundreds of men in the First World War. They are commemorated on a large cenotaph in Christchurch Park, which was unveiled in May 1924. Ipswich people had initially wanted to raise £5,000 for the memorial but in total over £50,000 was collected, enabling the surplus funds to go to Ipswich Hospital, who had cared for many thousands of injured servicemen. The low stone wall in front of the Cenotaph has bronze plaques that record the names of the dead. The names of those who died in the Second World War were added in 2004 and those from later conflicts are also being recorded.

The Cenotaph is located near an earlier memorial that was originally placed in the Cornhill but moved to the park in the early 1920s. This statue commemorates Suffolk soldiers who lost their lives in the Second Boer War of 1899–1902 and depicts a soldier in khaki uniform, bareheaded and standing with his rifle reversed, as at the graveside of a comrade. The sculptor of the bronze figure of a grieving soldier used for his model a soldier who had served in the South African war. This area of the park is the focus for the town's annual service of remembrance.

A fitting memorial to the fallen of the Second Boer War.

The restored and re-erected armillary sphere sundial.

A more recent memorial in Christchurch Park is an armillary sphere sundial, which was recently restored and relocated in the lower arboretum in memory of Dr John Blatchly who died in 2015. An armillary sphere is a model of objects in the sky consisting of a spherical framework of rings, centred on earth or the sun, that represent lines of celestial longitude and latitude and other astronomically important features. Dr Blatchly was a former headmaster of Ipswich School and a local historian. His research and writings on Suffolk and Ipswich contributed to, and enhanced, our knowledge of the history of the county and its county town.

Monopoly

In October 2006, Suffolk board game lovers welcomed the launch of a new edition of the popular Monopoly game. At first glance, this version looked the same as the usual board. However, on closer inspection, the familiar London squares such as the Strand, Bond Street and Piccadilly had been replaced by Ipswich locations such as Cornhill, the Waterfront and St Helen's Street. The aim of the game was the same as ever: players tried to develop their properties with houses and hotels, and then to collect rent from other players landing on their squares. According to a former Monopoly world champion, the three orange sites on any board are mathematically proven to give the best return. This is because when people go to jail – and anyone who has played the game knows this is quite often – a player must throw a 'double', which is more likely to total between six and nine, thus landing on an orange property. So, using this trick with the Ipswich edition, the most profitable places would be Bath Street, Tower Ramparts and the Buttermarket Shopping Centre.

Above: An imaginative substitute for the London railway stations.

Below: Was Ipswich Borough Council pleased with its place on the Monopoly board?

The Ipswich Monopoly board also features Ipswich Station and the (then) three park and ride sites at Bury Road, London Road and Martlesham instead of the London railway stations. Although over twenty separate editions existed before the Ipswich one, this was the first to have three football-related squares with the Alf Ramsey statue and the Bobby Robson statue joining Portman Road in the line-up. Unsurprisingly, Christchurch Mansion was the most expensive property, taking the place of the more familiar Mayfair. However, the cheapest property on the Ipswich board surprised many avid players. This was Grafton House, which was then the newly built borough council offices. When asked about this controversial choice, a spokesman said that they thought it best to put Grafton House on a moderately priced square because they knew how mindful the council was of spending taxpayers' money!

Museum Street

The curious resident or visitor to Ipswich may wonder why Museum Street is so called, since there is no museum located there. It is simply that the museum that was once there has since moved. The elegant building now housing a restaurant, Arlingtons, was designed as the first Ipswich Museum and opened in December 1847.

The Ipswich Museum, unlike similar institutions elsewhere, was to be for the benefit of the working classes so that they could learn about natural history. The *Suffolk*

The building after which Museum Street was named.

Chronicle, reporting on the new museum, described the wonders that awaited the public: 'The zoological specimens are so disposed as to exhibit to perfection the characteristics of the various animals, whilst the specimens in the ornithological department are likewise so placed as to form altogether a sense of great beauty.' Sadly, though, it seems that in the early years, a series of lectures that allowed free admission to those from the working class, were poorly attended by labourers. Also, entrance during the day was by subscription, although free entry was allowed on two evenings a week. The museum gained a national reputation under the control of a committee and its second president, Revd Henslow, who was a Cambridge professor and tutor of Charles Darwin. Over sixty leading scientists lent their support as honorary members or vice-presidents. Nevertheless, subscriptions were not enough to cover costs and the Ipswich Corporation took over its administration.

Eventually, Ipswich Museum was a great success and it was decided that the collection of natural history specimens should be housed in a bigger and more suitable environment. A new museum, together with a school of art, was designed by Horace Chesterton and opened in the High Street on 27 July 1881, at the same time as the new post office on the Cornhill and a new lock entrance to the wet dock. Today, the Ipswich Museum covers far more than natural history, although the Victorian purpose-built cabinets are still lined with exotic foreign animals arranged in their zoological classification. Many of the museum's rooms tell the story of Suffolk and its county town from pre-history to the present day in an engaging way, aimed at educating all ages.

This Victorian jewel still welcomes modern-day museum-goers.

Nelson, Horatio

For a town he only reportedly visited once, there are a number of references to Admiral Lord Horatio Nelson in Ipswich. Amazingly, Nelson had a home in Ipswich, on Rushmere Road, called Roundwood, but never stayed there. Instead, it was occupied by his wife and his father. Nevertheless, in 1800, the Borough of Ipswich granted Admiral Nelson the Office of High Steward, a prestigious, ceremonial appointment, in recognition of his naval achievements. In November of that year, Lord Nelson, together with Sir William and Lady Emma Hamilton (Nelson's mistress), arrived in Ipswich but found Nelson's house locked up and his wife in London awaiting his arrival. So, Nelson went to the Great White Horse for refreshment and rest before travelling onwards to London.

Many think that the Lord Nelson pub in Fore Street is so called because the famous admiral had stayed there, or at least visited. Sadly, he didn't. The inn merely changed its name in the early 1800s when Nelson was made High Steward of Ipswich. Before the name change it was called the Noah's Ark and is an inn that can trace its history

Below left: A watering hole for admirals.

Below right: Known as the Noah's Ark until the nineteenth century.

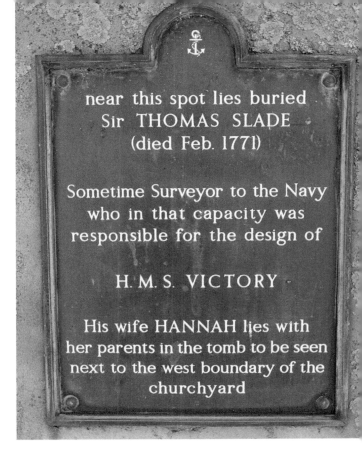

near this spot lies buried
Sir THOMAS SLADE
(died Feb. 1771)

Sometime Surveyor to the Navy
who in that capacity was
responsible for the design of

H. M. S. VICTORY

His wife HANNAH lies with
her parents in the tomb to be seen
next to the west boundary of the
churchyard

A great naval architect is buried in
St Clement's churchyard.

back to 1672. Aptly, the brick frontage was added in the twentieth century as a flood defence measure and, although the glazed bricks would not prevent interior flooding, they are built to withstand a short spell of immersion in water.

To the back of the Lord Nelson stands St Clement's Church. There is a memorial in the churchyard to Sir Thomas Slade who had designed Nelson's famous ship, HMS *Victory*. Slade was a qualified and experienced shipwright who had moved to Ipswich from London to work on ships commissioned to be built at the Ipswich shipyards. He married a local girl who he had buried in St Clement's, alongside her parents, eight years before his own death. When he died in 1771, his body was returned to Ipswich so that he could be buried alongside his wife.

Nonconformists

In the 1720s, the novelist Daniel Defoe toured the eastern counties and wrote an account of his journey. His religion was nonconformist, that is not Church of England, and so he often recorded the state of nonconformism in the places he visited. For Ipswich he says, 'There is one meeting house for the Presbyterians, one for Independents and one for the Quakers. The first is as large and as fine a building of that kind as most on this side of England, and the inside the best finished of any I have seen.'

The fine Presbyterian Meeting House Defoe describes is now the Unitarian Meeting House that stands in a courtyard off St Nicholas Street and Friars Street. It was built in 1699–1700 by Joseph Clark of Ipswich for just over £246 (excluding windows, galleries

Above left: The Unitarian Meeting House built by Joseph Clark.

Above right: The beer he received may have contributed to Clark's fine workmanship!

and internal fittings) and is still in use today. The contract for the works, which still survives, provides for 'four barrels of good small beer' for Clark and his workmen, which I am sure helped the project along! The restored interior today is much as it would have been when the meeting house was built, including box pews made of pine. In a few pews, there are wooden pegs, which are believed to be wig-pegs on which gentlemen could place their wigs whilst worshipping; these were still fashionable when the meeting house was opened. It also boasts a richly carved, hexagonal pulpit.

There were Quakers in Ipswich in the late 1600s and in 1700 Joseph Clark built them a meeting house in College Street at a cost of £200. In 1797 the property was enlarged. Many of the prominent families in the town worshipped in the Quaker Meeting House, including the Ransomes (ironfounders) and Alexanders (bankers). The College Street premises were sold off in 1924 and the adjoining burial ground walled off but retained and maintained. The Quakers now meet in a former private house.

O

Orphanage

Like all other urban areas of the country, Ipswich had its fair share of poverty in the Victorian era. At a time when the town was expanding with well-to-do suburbs, the authorities were struggling to support working-class families who were unable to provide for themselves. The 1834 Poor Law Amendment Act had established a system of workhouses designed as a deterrent rather than an attraction. It was a place of last resort when supporting themselves and their family through work was impossible. Inmates who entered the workhouse were housed in basic accommodation, given minimal food and made to do menial and repetitive work. The central authorities, though, believed that pauper children should be kept out of the workhouse whenever possible but relied almost entirely on private money to provide alternatives.

In 1873, Ipswich businessman and politician Edward Grimwade and his daughter Harriet Isham Grimwade established a privately run home, initially to take in women who were living a 'wicked and immoral' life. After a year, however, it was decided that

These gates offered entry into a new life for many orphans.

it would be best to provide a school for pauper girls who had been left motherless and who otherwise would have ended up in the workhouse. The establishment gained further local support and money, and in 1883 a purpose-built home was opened in Foxhall Road, which was named the Hope House Orphanage. It accommodated forty girls between the ages of three and ten. As well as three large dormitories for the girls, there was a sickroom, kitchen, dining room, schoolroom (in which they received elementary education) and other rooms needed for the running of the home. The orphans were lucky to have a large playground and garden in which to play. They were also trained for domestic service, taught how to make and mend clothes and to knit. The orphanage finally closed in around 1940 when it was sold and used to house members of the Women's Land Army in the Second World War. The building has now been converted into private residential accommodation.

River Orwell

Ipswich owes its existence and fortunes to the River Orwell. Without this wide, navigable waterway the port of Ipswich would not have been possible. The name Orwell is supposed to have derived from 'river near the shore' and is thought to be Anglo-Saxon in origin. Its source river, above the tidal limit at Stoke Bridge, is the River Gipping. The Orwell broadens into an estuary at Ipswich, where the seventh-century dock was established, and then flows out into the North Sea at Felixstowe after joining with the River Stour at Shotley. The Orwell has played its

The Orwell meets the Gipping near Stoke Bridge.

part in naval history from early times. In 1338 and 1339, Edward III assembled his fleet in the river before attacking France, and during the Second World War it was the scene of much naval activity.

The river's mudflats are an important habitat for a wide variety of wintering birds. The Orwell's estuary marks the southernmost point of the beautiful Suffolk Coast and Heaths Area of Outstanding Natural Beauty (AONB). This AONB was designated in 1970 in recognition of the important range of natural habitats and species contained within the region. The estuary is specially protected because of its national and international importance for wildlife. Many thousands of wintering waders and wildfowl depend on the food and habitat provided there. Among the sea lavender and common reed can be found redshank, lapwing, knot, curlew, dunlin, avocet, grey plover and many more birds who favour the salt marshes.

In 1979, construction started on a bridge designed to take the A14 (then the A45) to Felixstowe. Work was completed in December 1982 and, when opened, the Orwell Bridge was one of the largest continuous structures in the world. Its main span of 190 metres runs from the site of the former Ipswich Airport to Wherstead across the Orwell estuary.

The majestic Orwell Bridge in the spring sunshine.

P

Packard, Edward

Ipswich may well boast the dubious honour of having the only street in the country named after animal dung! In the 1840s, a botany professor at Cambridge University called Revd John Stevens Henslow discovered coprolites in the ground at various locations just outside Felixstowe. Coprolites are fossilised animal faeces and when Henslow examined their composition, he found that they comprised almost pure phosphate. He therefore patented an extraction process that involved dissolving the coprolite in sulphuric acid. The result was a valuable fertiliser, which was first produced by Edward Packard in his 'manure factory' in Ipswich docks in 1850. The street running along the north side of his works was named Coprolite Street. Today, the factory has disappeared and is now the site of the Neptune Marina apartment block.

Below left: The site of Edward Packard's manure factory.

Below right: The name Fison in one of its early incarnations.

In 1919, Edward Packard was joined in this successful fertiliser venture by James Fison. James was a member of the family that was one of the first British companies to produce malted barley for bakers and brewers. From 1849, Edward Fison Ltd had premises just to the south of Stoke Bridge, one of many buildings in the town converted into maltings. The red-brick construction had been used as infantry barracks in its early days. The Packard/Fison company flourished in the first half of the twentieth century and, by 1942, it had changed its name to Fisons Ltd. This Ipswich company went on to become a leading multinational pharmaceutical, scientific and horticultural chemical firm. It was listed on the London Stock Exchange and, at one time, was a constituent of the FTSE 100 Index. In 1995, Fisons was acquired by France's chemical giant Rhone-Poulenc.

Portman Road

Portman Road is probably the most famous street in Ipswich, nationally as well as internationally. This is, of course, due to it being the home of Ipswich Town Football Club, whose stadium bears the same name. As you might expect, Portman Road looks very different today than it did when it was created in the mid-nineteenth century, when it was known as Portman's Road. When the railway station opened in 1860, a road was needed to link the west side of the town with the station, and so Portman's Road was built partly across marshes. Portman's Road mirrored an older street perpendicular to it which was called Portman's Walk until the end of the twentieth century. It was renamed Sir Alf Ramsey Way shortly after the death of the East Anglian hero who managed the victorious England squad at the 1966 World Cup as well as managing Ipswich Town Football Club between 1955 and 1963.

It is perhaps fitting that Portman Road, representing the very best of Ipswich, should bear a name that harks back to the founding of the Borough of Ipswich. On 29 June 1200 townspeople gathered in the churchyard of St Mary-le-Tower to hear the reading of a royal charter that had been granted by King John. It gave Ipswich, then a busy port with a growing reputation for successful trade, the right to run their own affairs. The inhabitants elected twelve portmen who were to govern the town. These portmen were granted a meadow called Oldenholm on which they were able to graze their horses. Later the meadow became known as Portmen's Marsh, near where the football ground is today.

Portmen's Marsh today.

Public Health

Today we take our luxurious bathrooms for granted, but back in late Victorian Ipswich, the majority of working-class folk did not have their own toilet, let alone a bath. Vast numbers of the town's working population lived in The Potteries, an extensive area of terraced housing in St Clement's parish, to the north of Fore Street. These houses were packed close together and, to make conditions worse, many had additional people living in crudely constructed shelters in the shared back gardens. Water for cooking was drawn from a communal well that was often contaminated by the nearby shared toilet.

Like many of the main Ipswich employers, Felix Thonley Cobbold, of the famous brewing and banking family, was dependent on the health of his workforce for his continued success. He needed to depend on workers who were as free from illness as possible in order to maintain production and contribute to the turnover of the company. Cobbold could therefore see some advantage in ensuring that his employees took a weekly wash. He donated a piece of land and gave a £1,200 contribution towards the construction of Fore Street Baths, which opened in 1894. The distinctive building, with its porthole-style windows in the façade, held both a swimming pool and individual baths. Swimming pools were still a rarity in the late nineteenth century, although the Baths and Washhouses Act of 1846 had encouraged local authorities to fund the construction of washhouses for the working class.

The Fore Street Baths featured 'slipper baths', so called because unlike a domestic bath, they had a high end to lean against and were partially covered at the other end. This was for modesty and to keep the heat in. An attendant would fill the bath for a customer and frequently mothers and daughters would share a bath. Boys avoided a bath by swimming instead. Today, the building is still run by Ipswich Borough Council and is a popular recreational swimming venue.

A generous gift to the Victorian poor of the town.

Queen Elizabeth I

When Elizabeth I acceded to the throne in 1558 on the death of her half-sister, Mary, she returned the country to Protestantism. Elizabeth also set about promoting a feeling of unity and a sense of loyalty to their sovereign among her subjects. One of the key ways to achieve this was to be as visible as possible to as many people as she could, and the queen therefore embarked on a series of summer progresses to different parts of her realm.

In 1561, Elizabeth decided to visit Ipswich. Moving the queen around her realm was a logistical nightmare for her officials. Elizabeth and her close advisers rode on horseback, accompanied by between 200 and 300 horse-drawn carts, which carried everything necessary to establish the queen's personal chambers. Unfortunately, entertaining royal visitors was an expensive business and hosts were expected to foot the bill. In advance of Elizabeth's visit to Ipswich in August 1561, the borough decided to levy a tax on all householders to fund the extra outlay required. During this visit, Elizabeth stayed for almost a week at Christchurch Mansion. The priory on the Christchurch estate had been closed by Elizabeth's father, Henry VIII, and in 1546 a prominent London family,

Elizabeth I chose to stay at the best address in town.

the Withypolls, had bought it for £2,000. They demolished the priory and used much of the stone to build the mansion, remodelling the ponds and turning part of the estate into a deer park. Elizabeth I enjoyed deer hunting and no doubt took advantage of this facility during her stay. Edmund Withypoll clearly found the expense of entertaining the monarch too great a burden and asked the town authorities for financial assistance.

Queen Mary I

Sixteenth-century Ipswich was a prosperous town but, like the rest of the country, it experienced religious turmoil, as successive Tudor monarchs swung the national religion between Protestantism and Catholicism. Suffolk witnessed first-hand the accession of Mary I when she emerged triumphant from Framlingham Castle on 19 July 1553 and made her way back to London to claim her crown. Mary journeyed through Ipswich, where she was met by the bailiffs of the town, who presented her with eleven pounds sterling in gold and by some young boys who gave her a golden heart inscribed with the words, 'The Heart of the People'.

Mary's five-year reign, however, was overshadowed by her aggressive attempts to reverse the English Reformation and to return the country to Catholicism. In the process, she had many religious dissenters burned at the stake, including thirty from Suffolk, nine of whom were from Ipswich and who are, today, commemorated on the Martyrs' Memorial in Christchurch Park. The memorial was erected in 1903 and was funded by private subscription.

The first recorded execution by burning in Ipswich was in 1546. This was of a man called Kerby. A large crowd of many hundreds gathered on the Saturday to witness the event, which was held at the Cornhill (then called the Market Place). Adjacent was the meat market building called the 'shambles', a large timbered structure with an arcade around the ground floor, and with a balcony above from which public spectacles could be viewed. A large company, including most of the neighbouring justices, were assembled there, and the stake, broom and brushwood faggots had been set up in the centre of the Cornhill. Kerby was fastened to the stake with irons. From the balcony of the Shambles Dr Rugham, formerly a monk of Bury St Edmunds, delivered a sermon before Kerby was put to death.

A troubled era in English history is commemorated in Christchurch Park.

R

Ragged Schools

In the mid-nineteenth century, the town was bursting to the seams with working-class families who were moving to Ipswich to find employment. Sadly, some did not find jobs, and they and their children teetered on the breadline, the parents often turning to crime to make ends meet. However, these families were lucky to have in the town many wealthy men who believed in empowering the young to better themselves. In 1849, the Quaker banker Richard Dykes Alexander established a school for children 'too poor, too ragged, too filthy, too ignorant for ordinary instruction'. It was open to any child whose parents were considered worthless, common criminals or beggars.

A school for children 'too poor and too ragged'.

The successful Ragged School expanded in 1900.

The school was called the Ipswich Ragged School and soon after starting it moved into purpose-built premises in Waterworks Street. It was supported by wealthy private individuals who paid a subscription to keep the school running. For the first nineteen years Joshua George Newman was master of the Ragged School and, with the help of his wife and a few volunteers, taught the children to read and write. Boys were also taught carpentry and girls were instructed in domestic skills.

In 1870, when the Forster Elementary Education Act heralded state education for all children, the Ragged School became known as Waterworks Street Infants, although soon afterwards it was handed back to its owners who continued to run it as a Ragged School. In 1900, the school expanded into a new larger building up the road in Bond Street in which the infants and girls were educated. It was supported by the great and the good, marked by the various engraved stone plaques set into the brick wall. These included the then Member of Parliament for Ipswich D. Ford Goddard, the Mayor of Ipswich, W. F. Paul, the High Sheriff of Suffolk, Roger Kerrison, and the Marquis of Northampton, who was president of the national Ragged School Union.

Railway

The railway was relatively late in arriving in Suffolk compared with elsewhere in the country. Although the Grand Eastern Counties Railway had been formed in 1836 with the aim of providing a link from London to Norwich and Yarmouth via Colchester, due to opposition from various vested interests, the first steam locomotive did not cross into Suffolk until ten years later. This was made possible by a second company, set up by John Cobbold and his son, John Chevallier Cobbold, called the Eastern Counties Railway. The Colchester–Ipswich line was opened on 11 June 1846, the day declared a holiday, and the first train arriving in Ipswich was greeted by 600 ladies waving 'snowy kerchiefs'. In August 1846, the *Railway Times* proclaimed,

> The line from Colchester to Ipswich is a little wonder. This wonderful rapidity of operation has been carried on, in the face of difficulties which would have destroyed the energies of most men. For their great success the shareholders are undoubtedly mainly indebted to Mr J. C. Cobbold, their chairman. He has been a man of untiring energy in the cause which he has had at heart, and a long course of hard up-hill work he is deservedly reaping the fruit of his labours.

The first Ipswich station was called Ipswich Stoke Hill and was in Croft Street. Later, the tunnel through Stoke Hill was built and the station was relocated to its present site in 1860. A new road, Princes Street, was laid, which linked the station to the town. It was named after Queen Victoria's husband and Consort, Prince Albert, who had used this new form of transport to visit Ipswich on 3 July 1851. While in Ipswich he attended various lectures at the Mechanics' Institute and addressed a meeting of the British Association for the Advancement of Science. The streets were lined with crowds of people who clapped as the prince rode in his open carriage escorted by a detachment of Horse Guards. The following day, Albert attended more lectures and talks relating to agriculture, science and commerce before having lunch at the Crown and Anchor Hotel in Westgate Street.

Ipswich Station was built in 1860.

Self-improvement

In 1824, a progressive new establishment opened its doors in Ipswich. The Mechanics' Institution in the town was one of the first such organisations in the country dedicated to making scientific and technical knowledge available to working-class men as well as encouraging their general and vocational education. This was at a time when few labourers had an education, even though these workers were employed in the fast-paced industrial sector. A schoolroom in St Matthew's Church Lane was rented for 15 guineas a year and was kitted out with scientific equipment including a pair of globes, a prism, models of crystals, some ancient sculpture and more than 140 books. There were 222 members in the first year who were encouraged to improve their level of education by attending talks and reading suitable books. Among the main activities of the Mechanics' Institution in its early years were lectures on scientific subjects given by local men. There was even one talk given by a lady, although very few people attended as it was considered too daring at the time.

The Rep was built as a lecture theatre for the Mechanics' Institution.

The door of the Ipswich Institute leading off Tavern Street.

Such was the success of the Mechanics' Institution that, in 1834, it moved to Tavern Street, into a former chemist's shop that was able to house the growing library of books. Later a grand, purpose-built lecture theatre was constructed in Tower Street. However, by this stage, not many men from the working class were attending its events and it became more of a middle-class club. This was mainly due to a 'rival' establishment that had been set up by Revd F. Barham Zincke in the Old Assembly Rooms in Tavern Street. This was called the Ipswich Working Men's College and members paid an annual subscription to attend evening classes in subjects such as book-keeping, chemistry and foreign languages.

In 1893, the Mechanics' Institution formally dropped the word 'Mechanics' from its title and its successor, the Ipswich Institute, continues to this day in Tavern Street and in a newly acquired building in Tower Street. It is now a registered educational charity, open to all who pay an annual subscription. Members benefit from a well-stocked library as well as a wide variety of courses, lectures and trips. Self-improvement in Ipswich is therefore still alive and thriving in the twenty-first century.

Silent Street

Nobody actually knows how the intriguingly named old thoroughfare Silent Street got its name. However, eminent local historians have put forward some equally interesting theories. Silent Street hasn't always been called that. One of the earliest known names is Half Moon Street, possibly after a pub of the same name, which has long since disappeared. On John Ogilby's map of Ipswich dated 1674 – the first large, detailed, to-scale plan of the town – the area in which Silent Street sits was known

Were these houses full of plague victims?

as Colehill, with the road itself called Colehill Lane. There are also documents dating back to the early 1300s in which the Colehill in St Nicholas' parish is mentioned. Again, opinion is divided on the origins of this name. One theory is that it was the place where coal transported by ship from north-east England was put up for sale.

Back to the Silent Street named on Joseph Pennington's 1778 map, two possible reasons for the naming have been put forward. The first is that during the plague outbreak that spread to Ipswich from London in 1665–66, the street became eerily quiet due to the large number of deaths in the neighbourhood. Apart from the discrepancy between the date and the name of the street – in 1674 it was still called Colehill – it is hard to imagine that this road was harder hit in terms of plague victims than its neighbours. The second theory has more backers. The story centres on Curson House, which stood in the vicinity. During the wars with the Dutch in the second half of the seventeenth century, the house was used as a hospital for sick and wounded sailors. To ensure a speedy recovery in peace and quiet, it is said that straw was laid down in the street to deaden the sound of carts and horses, leading to the apt name.

So, which of these tales is correct, if any? Well, the reader is invited to choose their favourite story and stick to it.

Was straw once laid down in Silent Street?

Sport

Today when most people think of Ipswich and sport, they think of the successful Ipswich Town Football Club. Although association football's history stretches back before the advent of the town's team, Ipswich residents in earlier centuries enjoyed participating in, and spectating at, far more brutal sports. From medieval times, the Cornhill was the venue for the cruel sport of bull- and bear-baiting. A German visitor to this country in the late 1500s described the scene: 'In the middle, a large bear on the long rope was bound to a stake, then a number of great English mastiffs were brought in and shown first to the bear which they afterwards baited one after another. When the first mastiffs were tired, fresh ones were brought in to bait the bear. When the first bear was weary, another was supplied and fresh dogs to bait him, first one at a time, then more and more as it lasted, till they had overpowered the bear.' Back in 1468, the Ipswich authorities had decreed that a fine of 12 pence should be paid by any butcher who sold beef from bulls that had not been baited by dogs. It was thought that baiting improved the tenderness of the meat.

Another unpleasant sport enjoyed by our forebears was cockfighting. Publicans were among the first commercial sponsors of 'cocking' and the inns would make handsome profits from selling food and drink to the spectators until the sport was banned in 1795. Many Ipswich hostelries had cockpits where the gamecocks – specially

Above left: Bear-baiting was a popular spectator sport on the Cornhill.

Above right: The venue for cockfights in the eighteenth century.

bred for the purpose – would fight to the death. In the 1750s, a new cockpit was built at the Bear and Crown and in the following decade the appropriately named Cock & Pye hosted a match just after Christmas between cocks belonging to two sides – one team of gentlemen from Ipswich and one from elsewhere in the county. They brought thirty-one cocks each to stage a series of fights. The prize was two guineas per battle.

T

Tacket Street

'Tacket Street is now almost a plain street, but there were formerly situated, perhaps, the grandest mansions in the town.' This quote comes from a book written in 1888 by J. E. Taylor entitled *In and About Ancient Ipswich*. It gives us some tantalising clues into the street's history and tells us that the thoroughfare had already changed out of all recognition by the end of the nineteenth century. Sadly it is a shell of its former self today.

In 1553, Tacket Street was the focus of attention when Mary I stayed in the house of Robert Wingfield on her way back to London from Framlingham Castle to claim the throne of England. Although we know very little about other fine houses that stood in Tacket Street, visitors to Ipswich are still able to view part of the interior of Wingfield's house. The carved oak panelling and mantelpiece from its main room, 'The Great Parlour', are now in a room in Christchurch Mansion. In the 1730s, part of Wingfield's former residence was used for the Tankard Inn and the other part for the first permanent theatre in Ipswich. Both properties were owned by Henry Betts, a local brewer, and the inn was known for some time as the Theatre Tavern. The theatre closed

'Tacket Street is now almost a plain street'.

Wingfield's magnificent carved oak mantelpiece.

in 1890 and became a Salvation Army citadel. The Tankard Inn was finally demolished, with adjacent properties, to make way for the twentieth-century car park.

There is much debate among historians about the origins of the street name. During the eighteenth century, the road was called Tankard Street, but both before and after it bore its current name, possibly derived from 'tack' or 'tackle' – a term used in shipyards. It is likely that the Tankard Inn was named after the street rather than the other way around, but we shall never really know. What is almost certain is that the name reverted to Tacket Street on the insistence of the nonconformist church, which had been built there in 1720. It was thought that to be called 'Tankard Street Congregational Church' sent out the wrong message to would-be worshippers.

Tallest Building

With all the modern high-rise developments dotted around Ipswich, it is difficult to imagine the pre-twentieth-century skyline of the town. If you can visualise it, though, it would be dominated by church towers and spires. Many of these churches have been subject to substantial redesign and rebuilding projects across the centuries. For example, the tower of St Lawrence Church was restored in the 1880s when it was re-clad in flint and Portland stone. Its height is a mere 30 metres, dwarfed by the spire of nearby St Mary-le-Tower, which reaches 71 metres. The present church of St Mary-le-Tower is the fourth structure to stand on this site. The first, which was there when the Domesday Book was compiled in 1086, was probably built of wood. The second was a stone building in the Romanesque style, which had been built sometime before 1200 when the borough charter was received by the townspeople in its churchyard. We know this because this church is shown on the borough seal. In the mid-fifteenth century St Mary-le-Tower was rebuilt once again. This would, no doubt, have been a magnificent medieval church. However, this building only lasted 400 years.

Above left: St Mary-le-Tower has only recently been ousted as the town's tallest building.

Above right: Cranfield Mill soars above derelict warehouse buildings.

During this time it had had a spire, which was blown down in a hurricane on 18 February 1661. It had to wait until the nineteenth century to be reinstated. The church we see today was built in phases between 1850 and 1870.

One of the first major building booms in Ipswich was in the 1960s and '70s when the Greyfriars development was constructed. The project was not well received and many of the buildings were either demolished in the 1990s or were refurbished, including two high-rise blocks. Nevertheless, until 2009, the spire of St Mary-le-Tower remained the tallest structure in the town. It was then overtaken by the twenty-three-storey tower at Cranfield Mill on the Waterfront, which was intended to be the 'landmark' building in Ipswich, clad with white polystyrene tiles with splashes of primary colours. However, the development was beset by financial difficulties and the contractors went into administration. In October 2013, the empty building was hit by gale-force winds, which ripped some of the cladding from the façade. Finally, in early 2017, the first flats were completed and occupied.

Tooley, Henry

Until the medieval church of St Mary-at-the-Quay closed its doors in 1940, a rather unusual ceremony was enacted each Friday without fail. Remarkably, the same service had occurred every week since the sixteenth century. All the residents of the nearby Tooley's Almshouses were required to make their way to a tomb in the north transept of the church. There, an official would read the residents' names in turn and place one packet of money on the tomb for each resident. The residents would then claim a packet each. The tomb is that of Henry Tooley and his wife, Alice. Henry Tooley was a wealthy merchant and one of the portmen (governing officials) of Ipswich. Unusually for a Tudor woman, Alice was Henry's business partner, and the couple traded in cloth, grain and wine. They owned a large house and trading hall on St Mary's Quay.

By the time Henry Tooley died in 1551, he had amassed a considerable fortune. In his will, Tooley left a large sum of money for the setting-up of an almshouse, originally for ten poor people. Tooley's foundation was later joined with that of William Smart, another merchant and portman. He had made provision in his will of 1598 to support paupers in the town. The almshouses were in what is now called Foundation Street, named after the Tooley and Smart foundations. The buildings were completely rebuilt in 1846 in a mock-Elizabethan style, and there have been alterations and additions since. Residents of the present-day almshouses still benefit from the endowments of two of Ipswich's richest sixteenth-century philanthropists. Several plaques in gold, red and black paint on the relief mouldings ensure that the two men are not forgotten, as the wording includes the following verses: 'In powerfull Silence lett great Toolie rest; Whose charitable Deeds bespeak him blest' and 'Let gentle Smart sleep on in pious trust; Behold his charity, respect his dust'.

Tooley's tomb where his almshouse residents used to gather every week.

Victorian almshouses built to resemble the style of Henry Tooley's times.

Unicorn Brewery

You have to look very hard to find a unicorn. However, in Ipswich, high above your head, is one such beast, resplendent with its distinctive curly horn. It sits atop a weathervane on the former Unicorn Brewery, which occupies a site on the corner of Orwell Place and Foundation Street. Its origins are unknown, but it is possible that it was a D. P. Goddard who first established a brewery there, possibly attached to an existing public house called the Unicorn. In the *Ipswich Journal* of 27 November 1813, under the heading 'Unicorn, Orwell Place, Ipswich', Goddard, who describes himself as a brewer and brandy merchant, '... respectfully informs the public that he has fitted up a brewery for supplying private families with genuine fine ale, porter and table beer; he has likewise laid in a choice stock of British and Foreign Spirits, which he offers upon the lowest terms, wholesale and retail, for ready money'. By 1842, when it and its associated pubs and beerhouses were sold at auction, the brewery was clearly a well-established and profitable concern. It boasted a capacity of brewing up to 10,000 barrels a year.

A flying unicorn?

The Unicorn was a once-successful brewery and pub.

Sometime after 1855, Nathaniel Catchpole bought the brewery business and ran it successfully for the rest of the century under the name Catchpole & Co. In 1918, the company name was changed to the Unicorn Brewery Co. Ltd but only four years later the firm, comprising the brewery itself and no less than fifty-six public houses, was taken over by Tollemache's Ipswich Brewery Ltd and Cobbold & Co. While brewing was moved to the Cliff Brewery, a member of the Catchpole family started a mineral water bottling plant on the Unicorn site. Talbot & Co. Ltd also produced lemonade, ginger beer and cider. During the Second World War, when a large number of US servicemen were stationed in Suffolk, the firm was apparently awarded the franchise for selling Pepsi Cola. The former brewery and pub buildings are now swanky apartments.

University

On 1 August 2016, Suffolk had an independent university for the first time. The University of Suffolk, whose main campus is on the Waterfront in Ipswich, was established in 2007 as University Campus Suffolk. RMJM Architects were commissioned to design the Waterfront building – the flagship of the university's several properties – which includes three lecture theatres and thirty-four smaller teaching rooms as well as offices. This six-storey building, officially opened in 2011, was built at a cost of £21 million. Its roofline curves down away from the Waterfront, to the height of the Tudor buildings in nearby Fore Street.

Probably the most controversial architectural feature of the university is the sculpture that stands in the plaza outside the university building on the Waterfront.

The University of Suffolk occupies a prominent position on the Waterfront.

What? Where? Why? Who?

It is a giant question mark made from Portuguese marble and Uruguayan granite, which is one half of a two-art commission costing £200,000. The other was an LED light display on the concrete chimney towering over the Northern Campus (the old Suffolk College site), which stopped functioning in 2013. The installation of the 4-metre-high Waterfront sculpture created a lot of media interest as well as generated a debate on what public art should do. One Ipswich councillor said that the money would have been better spent on public toilets. In the sculpture's defence the university said, 'We are a university and we are about questioning, interrogating – we are curious. The question mark is about us looking to the future.'

V

Visitors

While travel guides as we know them today did not exist in the seventeenth and eighteenth centuries, it was the fashion back then to tour the country. Some now well-known accounts of visits to Ipswich in this era give us an insight into the town in a bygone age. Celia Fiennes visited Ipswich in 1698 and had a rather mixed view of it, saying 'This is a very clean town. Ipswich has 12 churches, their streets of a good size well pitched with small stones. Their market cross has good carving, the figure of justice carved and gilt. There are but 3 or 4 good houses in the town. The rest is much like the Colchester buildings, but it seems more shattered, and indeed the town looks a little disregarded.'

When Daniel Defoe visited Ipswich in the 1720s, the town was still trying to recover from a serious economic decline, having lost its cloth manufacturing, the coal trade and most of its shipbuilding business. Nevertheless, Defoe was clearly impressed, mentioning a 'physic garden' belonging to a local doctor and advocate of smallpox vaccination, Dr Beeston. In John Kirby's 1764 edition of *The Suffolk Traveller*, he wrote of Ipswich, 'One favourable circumstance is almost peculiar to this place, which is, that most of the better houses, even in the heart of the town, have convenient gardens adjoining to them, which make them more airy and healthy, as well as more pleasant and delightful.' Dr Beeston's was by far the best-known of such gardens in which he cultivated a wide range of rare and exotic plants as well as native British species. Today, Dr Beeston's garden is commemorated in the name of a rather bare thoroughfare nestled among modern office blocks. It is called Coytes Gardens after Dr Beeston's nephew, Dr William Coyte, who inherited the physic garden from his uncle in 1731.

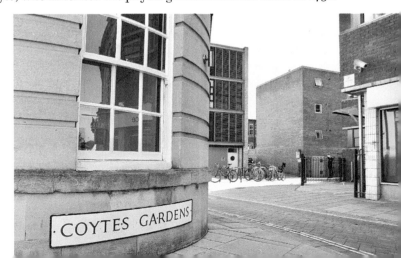

The site of a once-famous physic garden.

Wet Dock

Sitting on the now classy Waterfront, sipping a coffee (or something stronger) and looking out over the numerous yachts and motorboats moored on Haven and Neptune Marinas, it is easy to forget that this was a bustling, working port over many centuries.

At the end of the eighteenth century, Ipswich was still roughly the same size and shape as it had been in the early 1600s. However, all this changed rapidly in the early years of Queen Victoria's reign. Work had begun on the construction of a wet dock in the 1830s and when it opened in February 1842 at a cost of over £100,000, it was the second largest enclosed dock in the country with a total water area of 33 acres. Although the existing port facilities had allowed significant import of raw materials and export of manufactured goods, the silting up of the River Orwell meant that no large vessel was able to reach the quays. Therefore, the creation of this large basin and lock paved the way for the commercial and industrial success of the town. By the early

Yesterday a busy port, today a marina.

twentieth century, it was necessary to expand the area immediately outside the dock so that even bigger ships could access the port. The dock continued in use, though, until the development of the West Bank terminal in the 1970s, and at the beginning of the present century, commercial dockside buildings were gradually transformed into expensive residential developments.

What we now call the Old Custom House was built in the 1840s to replace a sixteenth-century timber-framed building with a colonnaded walkway along the front. The new-build was described by the *Ipswich Journal* at the time as 'a handsome building … capable of affording increased accommodation as a Custom House, sufficient

Ipswich continues a long tradition as a port.

The Old Custom House sits contentedly next to modern developments.

warehouse and other rooms for the business of wharfingers, an Excise office, and a coffee-room for captains of vessels and others connected with the shipping of the port'. In the twentieth century it was home to the Ipswich Dock Commission and now serves its successor, the Ipswich Port Authority.

Windows

Many of the finer architectural details of the town's buildings can only be appreciated by looking up. It is often surprising what you see if you look above the modern shopfronts with their corporate colours and logos. There is one feature that occurs in similar forms on several structures in central Ipswich dating from both the seventeenth and nineteenth centuries. It is a window with distinctive glazing bars, often in the form of a bay (or oriel) window on the upper floor. As well as the usual vertical and/or horizontal glazing bars, these windows have a small semicircle inserted at the top in the middle. The most impressive examples of this type of window can be seen on the Ancient House, but many other fine specimens survive, including on the former Wheatsheaf pub in Fore Street and the black and white building on the corner of Dial Lane and Tavern Street. This kind of window is found elsewhere in Suffolk and, indeed, was also incorporated in buildings in provincial towns in other parts of the country. However, architectural historians call this specific style the 'Ipswich window' and has pride of place in the textbooks alongside the similar 'Venetian window'.

The former Wheatsheaf pub boasts a fine example of an 'Ipswich window'.

'Ipswich windows' in the town centre.

Wolsey, Thomas

By the end of the fifteenth century, Ipswich was a bustling, thriving community with numerous churches, five monastic orders and four hospitals. The town centre was packed with markets and shops offering all manner of goods. Undoubtedly one of the most powerful men in England during the reign of Henry VIII was Thomas Wolsey, who was born in Ipswich in the early 1470s. Although he was often described as a butcher's son, Wolsey's father was probably a modest landowner who sold the livestock he reared on his land.

Thomas Wolsey benefitted from an education at Ipswich Grammar School, which, coupled with his intellect and ambition, enabled him to attend Oxford University followed by a rapid rise through the ranks of the Catholic church. In 1514, he was appointed Archbishop of York and a year later the Pope made him a cardinal. This was followed a month later by Henry VIII appointing him as Lord Chancellor of England, becoming the king's right-hand man. As one of the monarch's closest councillors, Thomas Wolsey became a rich man and, not forgetting his roots, he set about constructing a school for fifty boys in Ipswich, the College of St Mary, which opened in 1528. However, Cardinal Wolsey was stripped of his role as Lord Chancellor in 1529 and his property seized. His equally

The bronze statue of Cardinal Thomas Wolsey in St Peter's Street.

rapid fall from power was due to him enraging the king by not being able to secure a fast annulment for Henry of his marriage to Catherine of Aragon so that the king could marry Anne Boleyn. Wolsey died a year later.

Today, Ipswich's greatest son is commemorated across the town, including by a £90,000 bronze statue in St Peter's Street, which was unveiled in 2011 close to where Wolsey is believed to have lived as a boy. Nearby is the Thomas Wolsey pub, a beautiful seventeenth-century building, although only known by this name since September 2011.

Wolsey's name now also appears as a pub name.

X Marks the Spot

We are not lucky enough to have a treasure map marking the spot where Ipswich's castle used to stand. We know for certain that the town had a castle, but nobody knows exactly where it was as there is simply no trace of it on the ground or on any surviving, detailed maps (the earliest of which dates from the beginning of the seventeenth century). The castle was built sometime in the twelfth century by the Bigod family, who were the Earls of Norfolk and built their castles in the region. Although they had been favoured by William the Conqueror, the Bigods were members of a group of rebel barons under King Stephen. Stephen eventually besieged Ipswich and took the town and castle in 1153. The castle survived until 1176, when Henry II ordered its demolition along with other Bigod castles.

Did Ipswich castle once stand on this site?

The town's castle is likely to have been a Norman motte-and-bailey style of fortification, of which the most important element was the keep. The keep, possibly just made of timber, was built on a large, steep mound (the motte). The bailey sat at the base of the mound and contained ancillary buildings like the stables, kitchens and accommodation for the soldiers. The bailey was surrounded by a protective ditch and fence.

There are several theories as to the location of the castle, and the most compelling is that it sat on an area which, until recently, was known as the Mount. In the 1970s, a new Civic Centre was built on the Mount at the same time as Civic Drive was created. The centre served as home to Ipswich Borough Council for thirty-five years until it was demolished in 2009. The site is now a car park, and close by stands the New Wolsey Theatre.

Yew

The *Taxus baccata* or English Yew is frequently to be found in churchyards. Indeed, a number of the churches in Ipswich have yew trees growing close by and it is thought that the conifer was planted in churchyards as a resource for longbows, which were in great demand. In the Middle Ages, every able-bodied adult male in Britain was expected to be able to shoot a longbow, and thus be prepared to be called up to fight for his country. The yew is among the hardest of the softwood trees yet possessing elasticity – hence its suitability for these common weapons.

A yew tree that has witnessed many historic events.

The Round Pond was once used by monks as a fish pond.

Yew trees are one of the world's longest-lived species of tree; some examples in Britain are said to be over 1,000 years old. They are also slow-growing and are notoriously difficult to age. This is certainly true of the magnificent specimen in Christchurch Park, believed to be the oldest tree in the park. It stands over 14 metres tall and its trunk has a circumference of 447 cm. The Friends of Christchurch Park say that archaeological work has established that the yew is at least 600 years old. This would mean that it was planted in the time of the Augustinian Priory of the Holy Trinity (also known as Christ Church). The priory was established in the twelfth century with around 260 hectares of farmland. Nothing remains of the priory buildings that were dismantled in the sixteenth century when Christchurch Mansion was constructed.

As well as the ancient yew, several other features in Christchurch Park are said to date from the time of the priory. These are the Round Pond, the Wilderness Pond and a section of wall. The ponds may well have been used by the monks as fish ponds, providing the much-needed food for the monastic community. It is also thought that the park's springs supplied the town with water and were the source of some of the streams thar ran through the streets.

Zeppelins

During the First World War, Ipswich suffered two attacks from the dreaded German Zeppelin airships. Just after midnight on 30 April 1915, four bombs were dropped to the west of the town centre. The first two bombs fell on Barrack Corner and Waterloo Road but did little damage. Another bomb, however, set fire to houses in Brooks Hall Road. Luckily nobody was killed but one girl was injured. The second Zeppelin attack came on 31 March 1916. One bomb from the L15 airship fell, harmlessly, into the dock. Another, however, came through the roof of the Old Bull Inn on Key Street, behind the Old Custom House. It also destroyed the house next door to the pub, killing a man who was standing outside. A third bomb fell in Stoke Bathing Place, destroying the huts.

Coincidentally, some of the aircraft used during anti-Zeppelin patrols were built at Ransomes, Sims & Jefferies, based in Ipswich. Altogether, 790 aeroplanes were manufactured at premises at the Trinity Brickworks. It is believed that the first F.E.2b fighter plane built by the company was involved in the shooting down of the Zeppelin L48, which crashed at Theberton, near Aldeburgh, on 17 June 1917.

The Old Bull Inn was partly destroyed in a Zeppelin attack.

Bibliography

Bacon, N. and W. H. Richardson, *The Annalls of Ipswiche* (Ipswich: Private Circulation, 1884)

Bentley, James and Nikolaus Pevsner, *Suffolk: East: The Buildings of England* (London: Yale University Press, 2015)

Blatchly, John and Diarmaid MacCulloch, *Miracles in Lady Lane: The Ipswich Shrine at the Westgate* (Ipswich: J. M. Blatchly, 2013)

Defoe, Daniel, *Tour Through the Eastern Counties of England* (London: Cassel & Co., 1888)

Dymond, David and Edward Martin (eds), *An Historical Atlas of Suffolk* 3rd edition, revised and enlarged (Ipswich: The Archaeology Service, Suffolk County Council, 1999)

Field, Rachel, *The Ipswich Book of Days* (Stroud: The History Press, 2014)

Gardiner, Susan, *Ipswich Pubs* (Stroud: Amberley Publishing, 2016)

Gardiner, Susan, *Secret Ipswich* (Stroud: Amberley Publishing, 2015)

Hodges, Clive, *Cobbold & Kin: Life Stories from an East Anglian Family* (Woodbridge: The Boydell Press, 2014)

Ipswich from the First to the Third Millennium (Ipswich: The Ipswich Society, 2001)

Kirby, John, *A Suffolk Traveller*, 2nd edition (London: Longman, 1764)

La Rochefoucauld, François de, *A Frenchman's Year in Suffolk, 1784* (Woodbridge, The Boydell Press, 2011)

Malster, Robert, *A History of Ipswich* (Chichester: Phillimore, 2000)

Malster, Robert, *The Wharncliffe Companion to Ipswich: An A to Z of Local History* (Barsley: Wharncliffe Books, 2005)

Mugleston, Charles, *Charles Dickens in Ipswich* (Charles Dickens Theatre Company, 1983)

The Ipswich Maritime Trail (Ipswich: The Ipswich Society, 2017)

Twinch, Carol, *The History of Ipswich* (Derby: Breedon Books, 2008)

Twinch, Carol, *The Little Book of Suffolk* (Derby: Breedon Books, 2007)

www.eadt.co.uk

www.focp.org.uk

www.ipswich-lettering.co.uk

www.ipswichsociety.org.uk

www.ipswichstar.co.uk

About the Author

Although Sarah Doig was born in Hertfordshire, she considers herself a Suffolk girl. Sarah moved with her family first to Mildenhall when she was a year old and then to Bury St Edmunds where she was educated. Leaving Suffolk initially to attend university, Sarah found herself away from the county she considered her home for some twenty-seven years. After having travelled the world during her twenty-year career in the Foreign and Commonwealth Office, Sarah could no longer resist the strong pull back to East Anglia to which she returned in 2010. She now works as a freelance local history researcher, writer and speaker. Sarah's website is www.ancestral-heritage.co.uk.